CREATIVE WOODWORK

By the same author

METALWORK THEORY

Book One

Book Two

Book Three

Book Four

WOODWORK THEORY

Book One

Book Two

Book Three

Book Four

CREATIVE WOODWORK   P. F. Lye

HARRAP  LONDON

Acknowledgments

The author would like to thank the Governors of the Thomas More School, Purley for permission to include work done by the pupils of that school.

First published in Great Britain 1974 by
GEORGE G. HARRAP & CO LTD
182 High Holborn, London WC1V 7AX

Reprinted 1977; 1979

© P. F. Lye

ISBN 0 245 53168 8

*Printed and bound in Great Britain by
Redwood Burn Limited
Trowbridge & Esher*

Contents

Preface

Any casual observer of the human race or any serious student of history will certainly notice that from prehistoric times and in all environments human beings have enjoyed creating objects of art and beauty. Many of these creations produced through the ages and in recent times are the fruit of hard work and long experience based on a natural genius. But it is well to remember that they may be the end product of a process which had quite simple primitive beginnings.

Creative activity is enjoyable and it may be justified on this ground alone. It is enjoyable for the creator who derives satisfaction from the challenge and the struggle and more especially from the completion. It is enjoyable for all others when completed.

All constructions must, in the design process, take into consideration the qualities of the material used. In this book we are concerned with wood as the medium for our work. It is a very suitable medium being generally neither too soft for satisfactory work nor too hard for reasonably easy work. Within the medium there is a considerable range of hard or soft woods that we may choose from. It is even possible to choose woods having different qualities of texture, durability, colour or even cost to suit our needs. However, when using wood the natural structure of the material must be always borne in mind.

Wood, being composed of cells set up in tubular fibres, has a 'grain' structure which greatly affects the strength and working properties. Thus a piece of wood is strong along the grain but weak and brittle across the grain. This must constantly affect the design. Wood can be shaved with a plane or chisel along the grain, but it is much more difficult to work or to smooth on end grain. In addition many hardwoods suitable for carving often have twisted grain caused by the manner of the tree's growth. This can often be used to great advantage but to do so requires thought.

No one is an isolated unit working on his own. Each individual is obliged to accept some heritage which he may modify and improve and pass on. The same applies with creative work. Each individual cannot but accept ideas and techniques from others in his society. With the great expansion in communications in modern times we can accept influences from all parts of the world and we can even compare the work of different cultures. However, having accepted all these rich influences, each separate individual has his own personal contribution to make and make it he should.

The author has for several years past attempted to produce this individual contribution from secondary school pupils and some of the results are shown in the pages that follow. Inevitably the main influence that has been brought to bear on these young people is that of the teacher, but it is to be hoped that some wider influences may also be seen since the pupils have access to a wide variety of books and are encouraged to delve into their own experience.

The work included falls mainly into two categories—carving and modelling. Carving is the art of removing or subtracting material from a solid block to produce the required shape. Modelling is the art of building up or adding material to produce what is required. There is, of course, no reason why the two should not be combined.

Very few people can work directly on to the material of the project without extensive preliminary sketching or the construction of mock-ups in clay or one of the forms of rigid cellular polyurethane now available. It is difficult to think in three dimensions and unfortunately the use of sketches may add to this difficulty.

Every creator has a design problem. He has to decide what he wants to make and what form it should take. Wood carving particularly is a very personal expression and this accounts for so much of the satisfaction the accomplishment produces; but in general most people require some sort of a springboard. The sources of inspiration are limitless. When the whole field of animal and plant creation has been exhausted we can still find inspiration from human creations or employments. We still have the fertile fields of fantasy and the abstract. To be honest the creator is frequently limited by the material available.

MAKING A CARVING

Making a Carving

No two pieces of wood are the same. The process of making a carving will therefore follow a number of stages. Firstly a general idea of what is to be made is considered and this is followed by a search for a suitable piece of wood. When the wood is found there will be reconsideration of the design to suit the wood. These two major hurdles having been partially overcome there will then be detailed consideration concerning the degree of simplicity or complication to be attempted.

Consider a simple animal form such as a squirrel, weasel or marten. This form can be kept extremely simple as shown.

The design shown here is virtually a two dimensional cut-out. Any detail such as ears, tail or feet have been ruthlessly ignored—but the form remains and, if shaped and smoothed, can be an attractive ornament.

SIMPLE OUTLINE

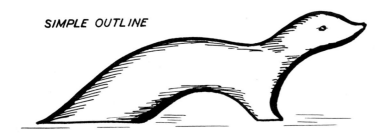

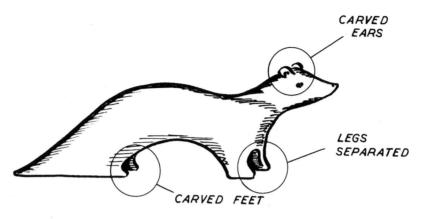

CARVED EARS

LEGS SEPARATED

CARVED FEET

Perhaps we would like to add a little more detail to the same basic shape shown on the previous page. We can add some carved ears and these, although not difficult to form, add a great deal to the head. We could perhaps carve an eye instead of inserting a bead. The front legs can be separated completely or halfway up and feet can be formed on the front and back legs.

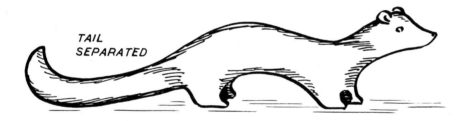

TAIL SEPARATED

The upper drawing here still shows an extremely simple carving though a little more detail has now been added. One of the main features of this type of animal — the tail — has so far been ignored and we may now wish to include this. It may be included as shown as a straight tail or curved over, possibly to touch the back of the body.

TAIL CURLED

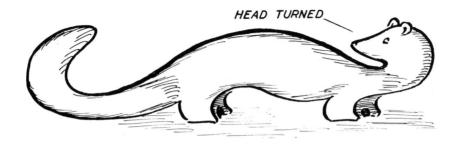

HEAD TURNED

All the designs so far considered are simple and rather lacking in 'life'. Perhaps we can introduce a little 'movement', say, by turning the head round. The head here has been turned right round so that the animal is looking directly backwards and we are still, therefore, working basically in two dimensions. It is not until we bring in some movement sideways — e.g., a sideways movement of the tail, a sideways twist to the

HEAD LOOKING SIDEWAYS

CURLED TAIL

body, or a sideways facing direction of the head — that we really begin to work in three dimensions. It is at this stage that the complications begin. Our pencil and paper become of rather less value. We can of course do quite a lot with pencil and paper particularly if we draw views from above or below. If we do not feel sufficiently confident to work directly on to the wood we may wish to do a mock-up in clay or some other soft material.

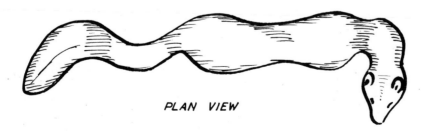

PLAN VIEW

13

If the wood being used is not more than 50 mm thick it is possible to cut away much of the waste with a bow saw. Wherever possible an extension of waste wood should be left attached to the main body until the work is completed. This provides something to hold it by, either in the vice or on the bench. Rounded work will always mark if gripped in the vice. When using a chisel remember that some woods split very easily along the grain.

Most amateur carvers smooth the surface of their work. One needs to be quite expert with the use of a gouge in order to leave work with the gouge marks on. This being so, any deep cuts into the wood should be avoided as these cannot be smoothed later with files and glasspaper.

When finishing a carving with glasspaper or garnet paper the final strokes should be along the direction of the grain. Glasspaper used across the grain will leave scratches. These small scratches are less likely to form when the movement is along the grain and they are less visible as they blend with the grain.

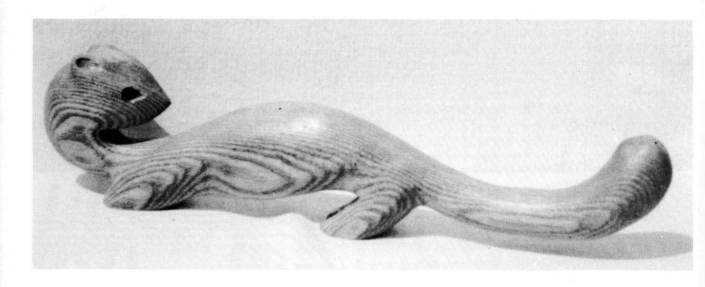

Many carvers advise the use of melted wax as a finish to the carving and this may work well with some dense woods. However, most wood absorbs wax much more on the end grain and this produces an uneven finish. In practice it is a good idea to seal the wood before waxing. The wood may be sealed by giving a coat of clear lacquer. Wood with a very absorbent end grain might require two coats. When fully dry the work is smoothed down with steel wool and waxed. Some people use the wax and the steel wool together.

CARVINGS OF SMALL ANIMALS—EXAMPLES AND DRAWINGS

TEETH
FITTED
AFTER
CARVING

18

ABOVE The work shows the carving of two fourteen-year-old boys both starting together with the same original idea.

BELOW Two carvings of ferrets, the work of sixth formers doing recreational woodwork. The pair are cut from one piece of beech, the single one was made by another pupil in the same group.

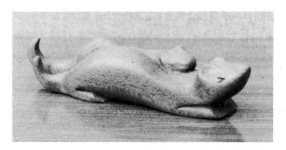

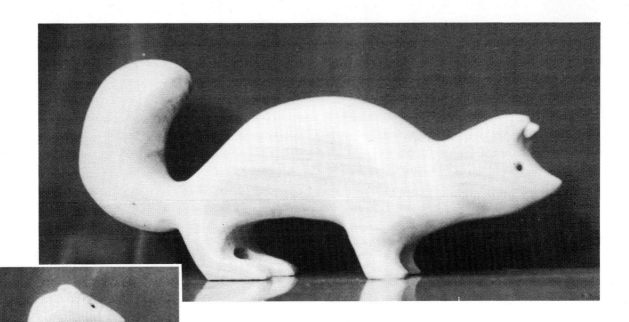

ABOVE The carving is of a squirrel designed and made in ash by a fourteen-year-old boy.

LEFT A carving of a stoat made by the author working with the same group of pupils. It is also made in ash.

20

ABOVE The carvings are made in ash and represent the design and work of two pupils working together with the same idea.

RIGHT An attempt at a squirrel eating a nut, by a pupil in the same group.

BELOW Stoats also carved in ash.

TOP Simple animal forms carved by the author working with twelve- to fourteen-year-old boys.

MIDDLE RIGHT Part of the CSE course of two fifth form boys.

LEFT A small animal form carved in elm.

BELOW A pair of stoats carved in ash.

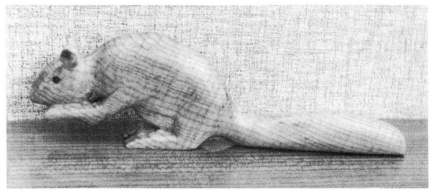

TOP A carving inspired by a beaver.

MIDDLE A squirrel. Stability is given to the carving by the long and rather heavy tail.

LEFT Barking dog.

The rabbit was designed and carved by a fourteen-year-old boy. The wood used is maple.

The cat stands about 450 mm tall and formed part of the CSE course work of a fifth form pupil. The wood used is elm.

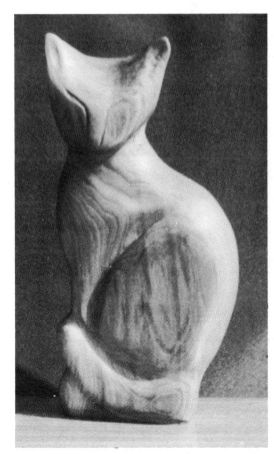

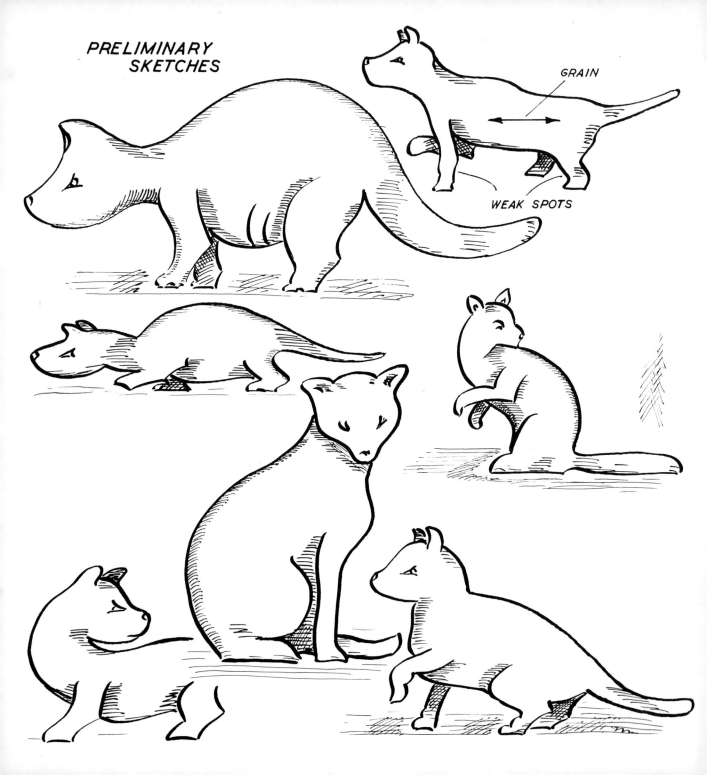

PRELIMINARY
SKETCHES

GRAIN

WEAK SPOTS

ABOVE A cat carved in ash.

BELOW A creeping cat carved in ash. This is one of several similar feline forms carved by a fifth form group.

The examples show a variety of feline forms. The eyes consist of a small bead set into a countersunk hole.

BUILT-UP MODELS

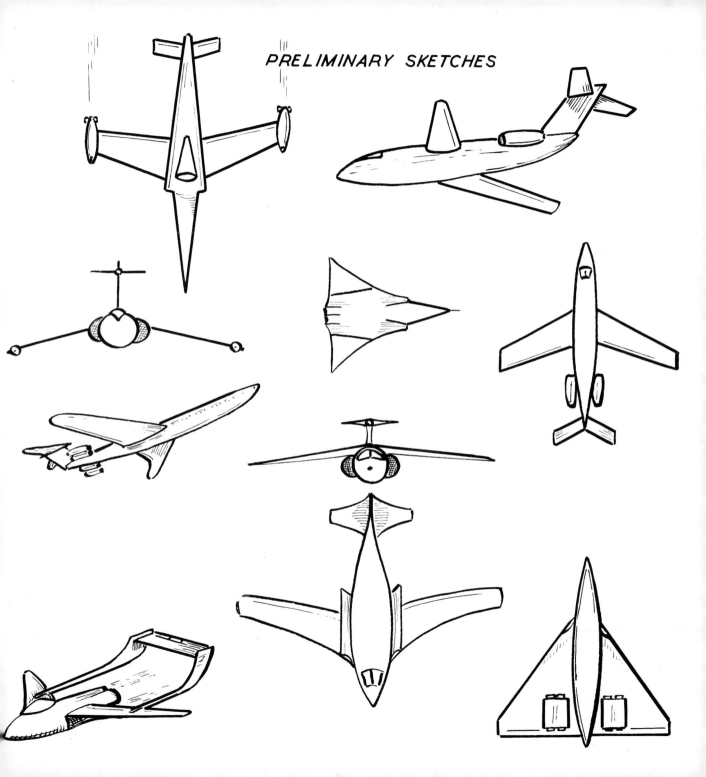

PRELIMINARY SKETCHES

The making of model aeroplanes can offer an interesting exercise in design. The approach can be technical or imaginative, traditional, modern or futuristic. The example above was based on a Hawker Siddeley 125 executive jet. The one on the right is an English Electric Lightning. The design below is from the memory and imagination.

The models require careful planning and can be built up from odd ends of softwood. Minor defects can be filled with a cellulose filler before painting and decorating.

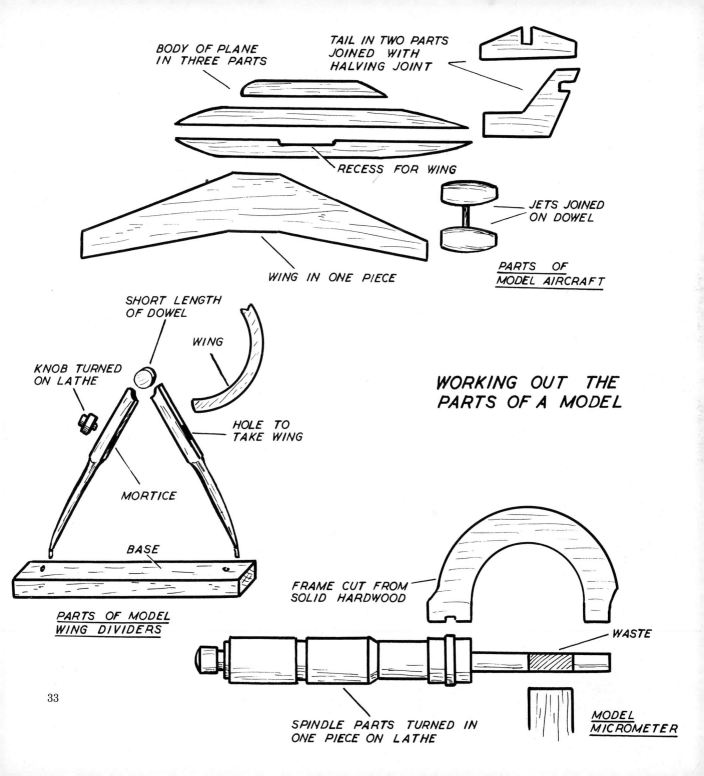

BODY OF PLANE
IN THREE PARTS

TAIL IN TWO PARTS
JOINED WITH
HALVING JOINT

RECESS FOR WING

JETS JOINED
ON DOWEL

WING IN ONE PIECE

PARTS OF
MODEL AIRCRAFT

SHORT LENGTH
OF DOWEL

WING

KNOB TURNED
ON LATHE

HOLE TO
TAKE WING

WORKING OUT THE
PARTS OF A MODEL

MORTICE

BASE

PARTS OF MODEL
WING DIVIDERS

FRAME CUT FROM
SOLID HARDWOOD

WASTE

SPINDLE PARTS TURNED IN
ONE PIECE ON LATHE

MODEL
MICROMETER

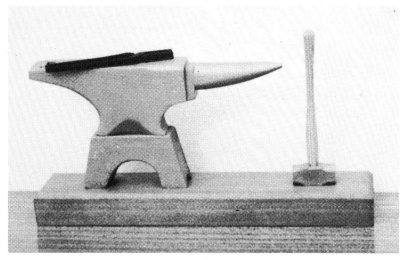

The models shown are made up from small oddments of hardwood glued together, the metal parts being sprayed with metallic paint and the whole then being mounted on a polished wood base.

The theme here was 'Occupations' and represented are Blacksmithing, Engineering, Navigation and Mechanics.

FISH AND BIRD CARVINGS

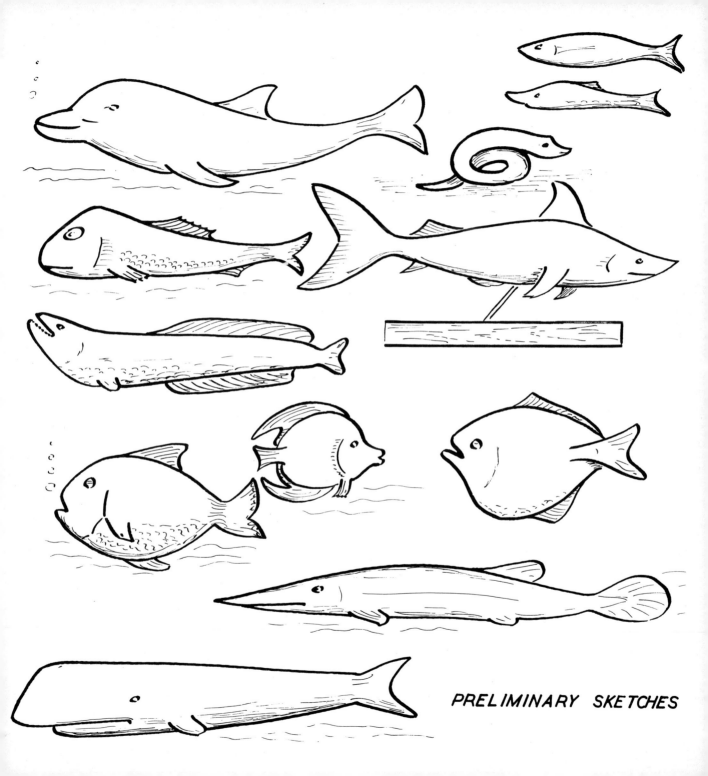

PRELIMINARY SKETCHES

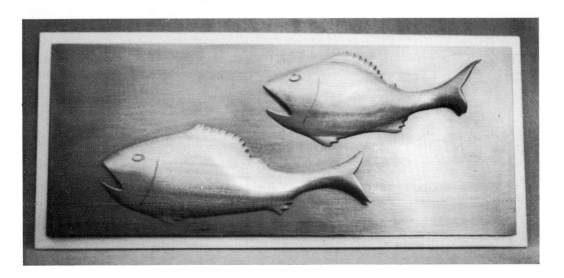

The examples show a variety of plaques. The fish are carved out and mounted on a board with provision for hanging on a wall. The upper ones are made in sapele and mounted on an ebonized board with a silver-blue surround. The lowest one is carved in beech and mounted on polished oak.

38

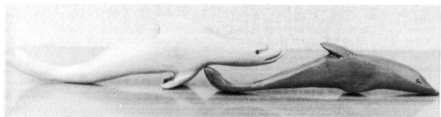

The examples show fish carvings made by fourth and fifth form pupils.

The carving of fish offers a very wide choice. Not only is there a very great variety of fish to copy but the imagination may also be used to produce an endless variety of fish forms.

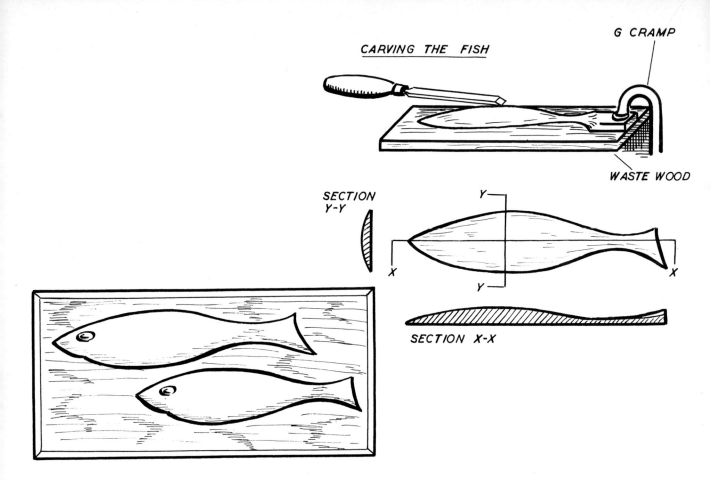

Carving a Fish

Fish are quite easy to carve. One of the possible advantages of choosing to carve fish is that there is such an extraordinary variety of shapes to choose from. It is possible to work entirely from the imagination in the sure knowledge that somewhere there exists a fish which resembles the image.

The design of the fish shown above has been simplified completely. Using this basic shape simplification can be effective, but clearly with some fish the fins—especially the dorsal fin—form an essential part of the characteristic shape.

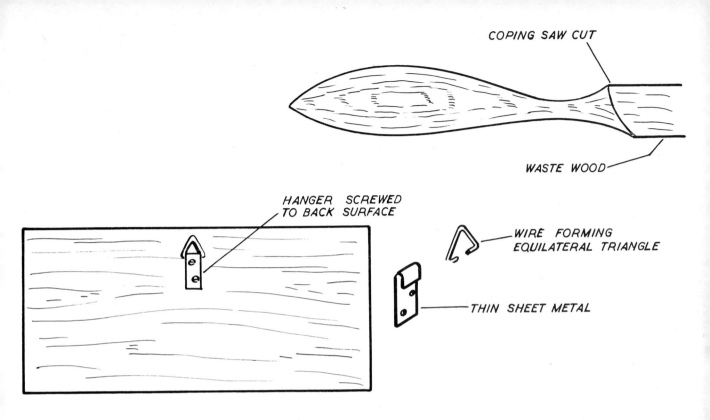

The disadvantage of carving fish is, of course, that fish do not stand naturally and any form of suspension or fixture tends to spoil the carving. It is reasonably successful to carve the fish in the form of a plaque as shown which can then be hung on a wall.

When carving the fish it is always advisable to leave an extension of waste wood preferably on the tail until the work is completed. This allows the work to be securely held without damaging the carving.

With many fish the junction of the tail and the body is slender and could therefore break quite easily when carved in wood. The tail itself can be made to look more lively if made to flick over at the top or the bottom. The fish should be completely finished before attaching to a back board otherwise it would not be possible to smooth the edges of the fish without scratching the board.

A small hanger as shown made from wire and thin sheet metal or flexible plastic should be attached to the board before fixing on the fish.

PRELIMINARY SKETCHES

BEAK CARVED & FITTED SEPARATELY

GRAIN

GRAIN

LEGS CARVED & JOINED TO BODY

BEAK JOINED FOR STRENGTH

GRAIN

GRAIN

GRAIN

GRAIN

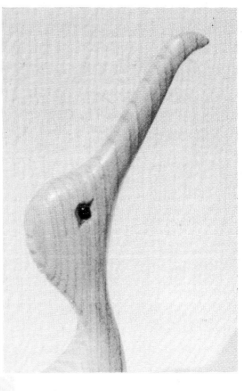

ABOVE A pair of cormorants made from ash, they stand about 300 mm high.

RIGHT ABOVE shows detail of the head and beady eye.

RIGHT A rather sad looking kiwi carved from an off-cut of dark red wood. It is rather unstable.

LEFT A very simplified kiwi clearly shows the grain taken along the beak to give strength.

BELOW LEFT A heron carved in ash by a fifth form pupil. On completion it was too unstable and was fitted to a larger base.

BELOW RIGHT A flamingo carved in beech. The bird and the base are one piece of wood.

44

ABOVE Two owls. The one on the left is the work of a thirteen-year-old pupil and carved in softwood, the one on the right being carved in teak by an older boy

RIGHT A long-eared owl carved in teak which formed part of the CSE course work of a fifth form pupil.

BELOW A long-eared owl carved in beech by a fifth form pupil.

ABOVE A goose and a hen carved in ash, the work of two fifth form pupils. The base of the hen is one piece with the carving, the pupil making the goose preferred to make a separate base with wood of a contrasting colour.

LEFT A woodpecker designed and carved in ash by a thirteen-year-old boy.

LARGER ANIMAL CARVINGS

PRELIMINARY SKETCHES

GRAIN

GRAIN

ABOVE The bears are carved in figured oak. As this wood has a very open texture it was treated with a filler before polishing.

LEFT The elephant is the work of a CSE candidate and stands about 250 mm high. It is carved in ash.

BELOW The rabbit is made in softwood by a twelve-year-old boy.

Kangaroos carved in ash.

PRELIMINARY SKETCHES

52

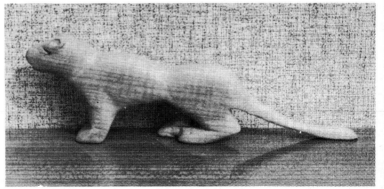

ABOVE Grant's gazelle made in beech by the author working with fifth form pupils.

ABOVE RIGHT A stag made by a fifth form pupil working with ash. The sapwood came through the animal's face.

BELOW RIGHT A lion designed and carved in ash by a thirteen-year-old boy.

ABOVE LEFT and RIGHT The work of two pupils in the same group. The wood used was kiln dried elm which proved to be rather brittle for the designs used.

RIGHT A deer carved by the author when working with fourth form pupils. The carving stands about 250 mm high and 320 mm long.

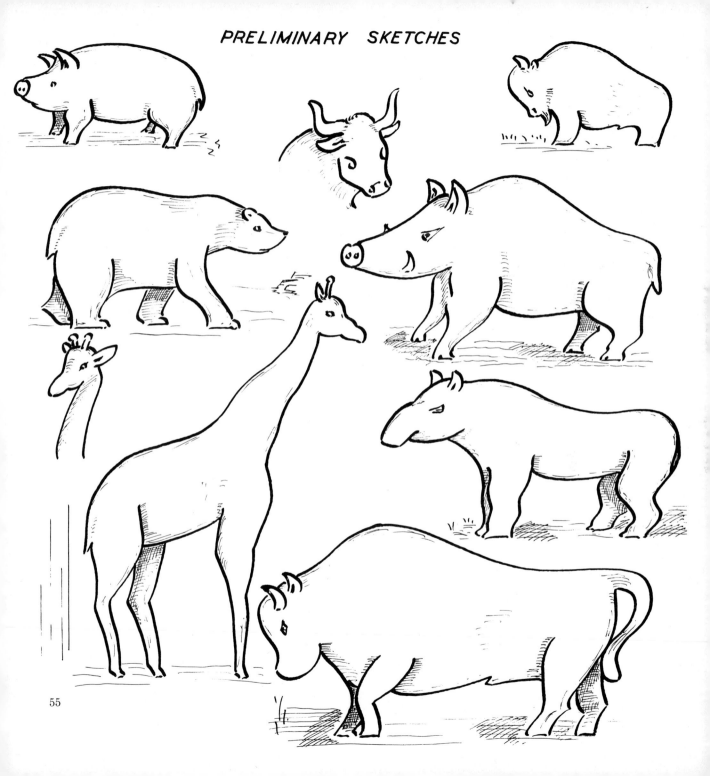

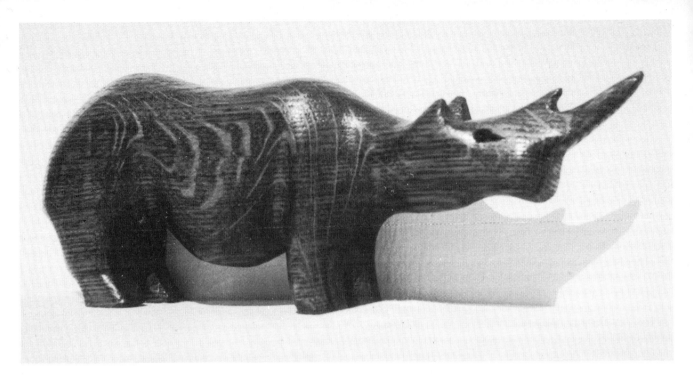

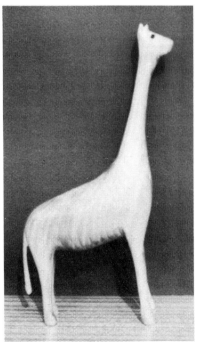

ABOVE A rhino carved in figured oak. It is about 300 mm long, 100 mm tall and 55 mm thick. When fully smoothed the wood was filled with a 'natural' filler before final smoothing with fine garnet paper. It was given a coat of clear lacquer, smoothed with fine steel wool and waxed.

LEFT The rather elegant giraffe was entirely designed and made by a thirteen-year-old boy. It was made from a very hard piece of ash and was smoothed and finished with great patience by the boy at home.

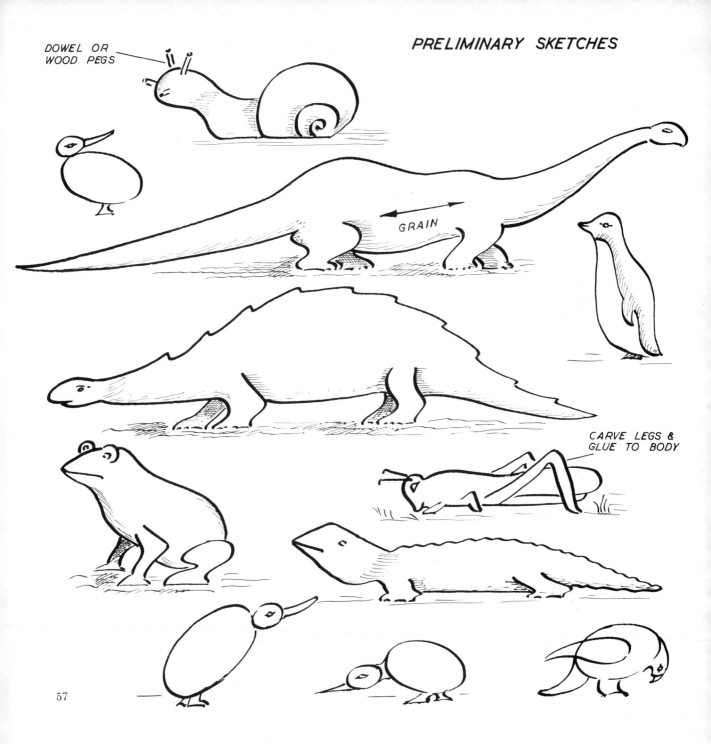

DOWEL OR
WOOD PEGS

GRAIN

CARVE LEGS &
GLUE TO BODY

ABOVE A large dinosaur carved in ash which measures about 600 mm long.

LEFT and BELOW Two snails made by fifth form pupils. The work combines lathe turning with simple carving and in each case the shell is made up of different coloured woods.

BELOW RIGHT Some models carved using off-cuts of African mahogany, the work of first year pupils aged about 11–12.

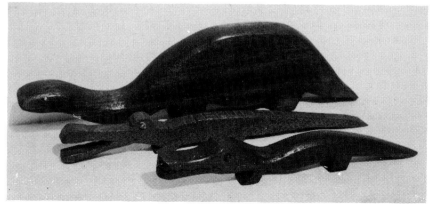

CARVING THE HUMAN FIGURE

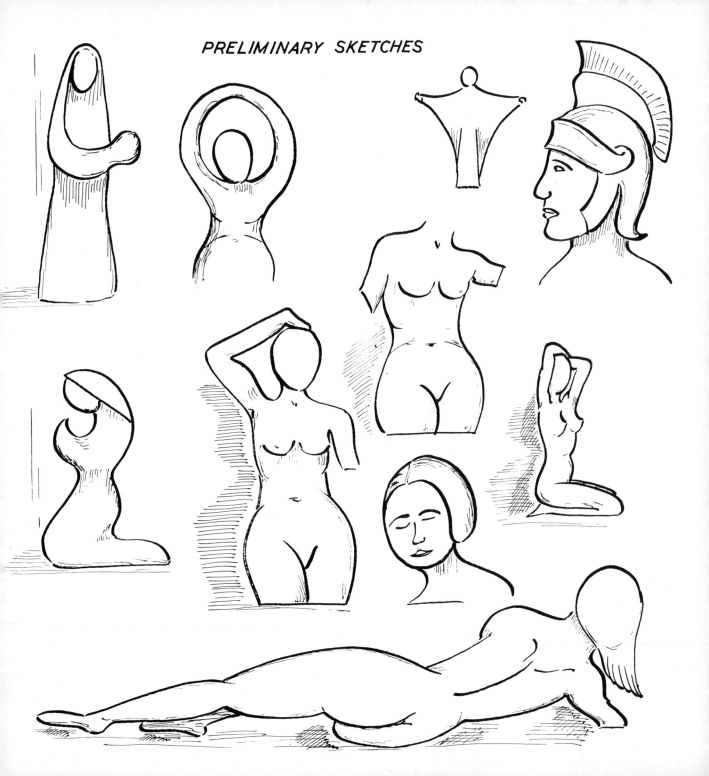

A crucifix carved in lime. The figure is made from two pieces joined by a halving joint and the joint is visible on the shoulder. Although considerable detail is included the figure is only about 300 mm high. The figure is left the natural colour of the wood, the cross is made of hardwood and painted blue with a matt finish, the halo is gilt.

LEFT The statue is carved in chestnut and is the work of a twenty-year-old student. It is made up from several pieces, the body, cape and dragon from one piece, the wings are each made separately, the shield is a separate piece as also is the lance, the whole being mounted on a large block for the base. The figure stands about 750 mm tall.

BELOW A pair of semi-abstract figures. The figure on the left inspired by a woman wearing a head scarf is carved in Douglas fir. The figure on the right carved in teak is inspired by a 'Madonna and Child'.

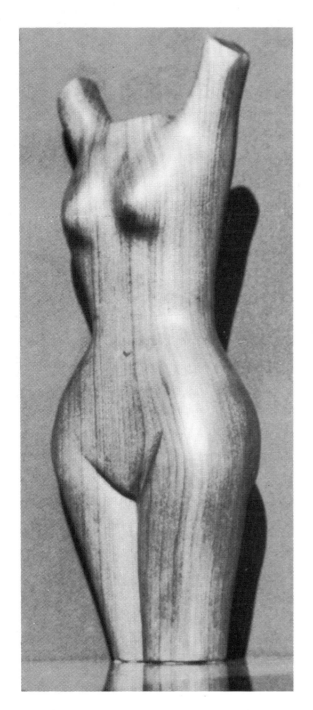

Torsos carved, below, in utile and in teak on the left.

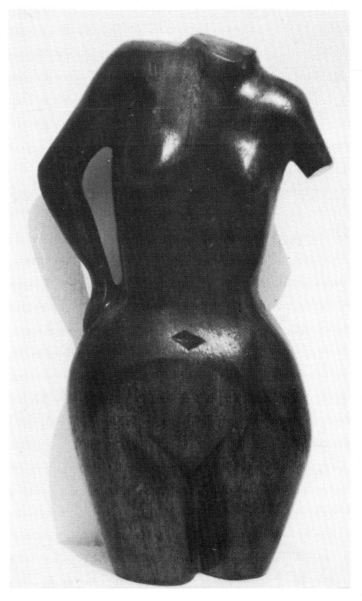

The rather 'oriental' figure formed the greater part of the CSE course work of a fifth form pupil. The wood used is teak and it was part of a very old gatepost salvaged in the demolition of a house. The figure is about 600 mm tall and 250 mm wide and deep.

ABOVE The torso also made in teak formed part of the same post. A defect in the wood made it necessary to cut out the centre and a join is visible unfortunately.

65

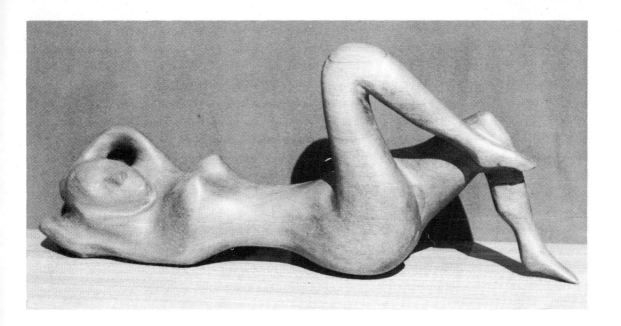

The preliminary sketch here shows a reclining figure 'Sun Worshipper' designed to be made as a pierced panel rather similar to the ones shown in the following pages. The photograph shows the same idea converted into a three dimensional carving. The wood used for the carving was African walnut (Lovoa).

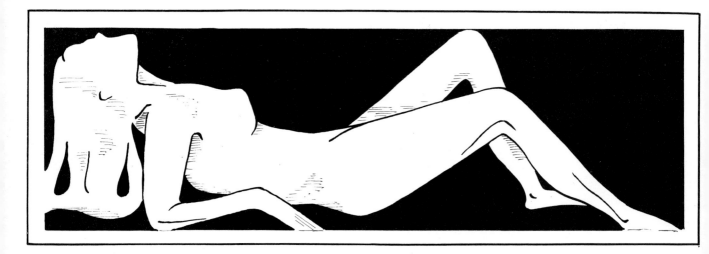

ABSTRACT AND REPRESENTATIONAL WORK

PRELIMINARY SKETCHES

The making of pierced panels offers a very fertile field for the working of fantasy and representational art forms.

ABOVE A carving made in the negative and inspired by a seagull swooping. It is the work of a fifth form pupil and is carved in abura 16 mm thick.

LEFT 'Education' carved by the author. The larger figure has the headgear of a monk or nun to indicate dedication. One hand in the positive is held out in explanation, the other hand in the negative embraces the pupil. The upward gazing pupil holds a book and although it was not intended to have wings the figure has an angelic suggestion. The panel is in utile 22 mm thick and about 750 mm tall.

ving re-
made in
he work
tow An
dge and
surface
ricately
fantasy
made in

71

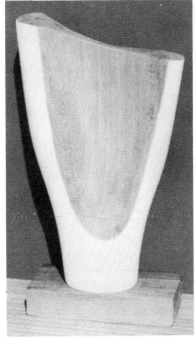

ABOVE A pierced panel carving 'The Monster' in African mahogany 22 mm thick. The panels on this page are backed with leather cloth.

RIGHT A panel inspired by chess pieces.

FAR RIGHT A pierced panel showing a skunk doing its characteristic handstand.

ABOVE FAR RIGHT An abstract carved in elm the outer surface being contrasted with silk finish white paint.

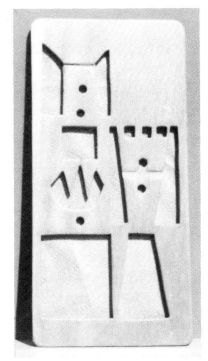

73

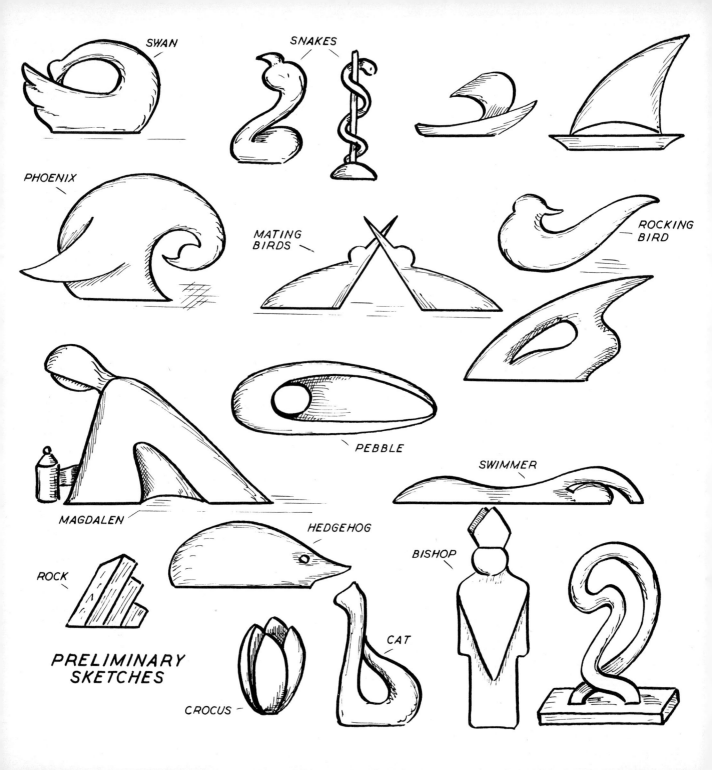

SWAN

SNAKES

PHOENIX

MATING
BIRDS

ROCKING
BIRD

PEBBLE

MAGDALEN

SWIMMER

ROCK

HEDGEHOG

BISHOP

PRELIMINARY
SKETCHES

CROCUS

CAT

RIGHT An example of abstract carving working with off-cuts of ash. The carving has been dictated by the grain of the wood which contained a large knot deeply split.

BELOW An attempt to produce a 'touch' ornament. It is made in teak and a very smooth waxed finish was obtained. It is the work of a fifth form pupil.

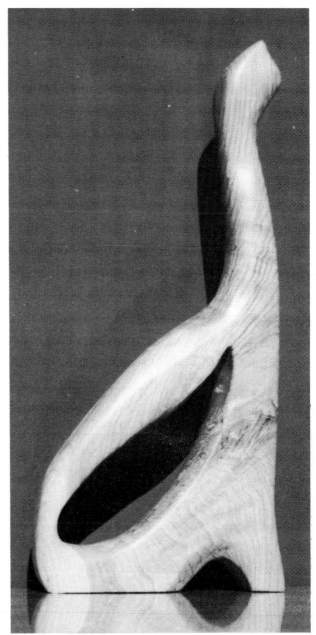

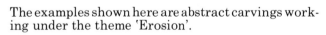

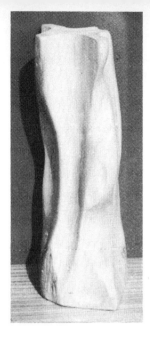

The examples shown here are abstract carvings working under the theme 'Erosion'.

ABOVE and RIGHT are two views of a carving in teak which stands about 300 mm tall.

TOP RIGHT is a fairly simple form in maple.

76

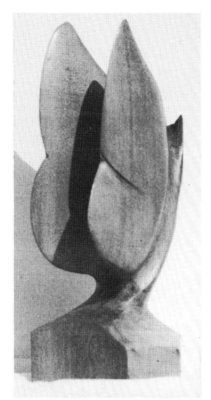

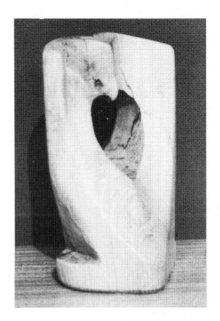

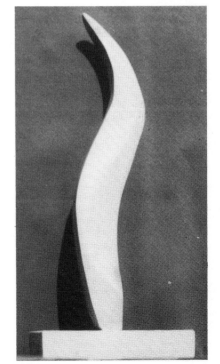

ABOVE Two views of a moth or butterfly carved in maple.

ABOVE RIGHT A heart within a heart. An abstract carving made from a rather rough piece of maple by a fourth form pupil.

BELOW RIGHT 'Blowing in the Wind'. An abstract carved in maple by a fourth form pupil and mounted on a separate base.

LAMP BASES AS A VEHICLE FOR CARVING

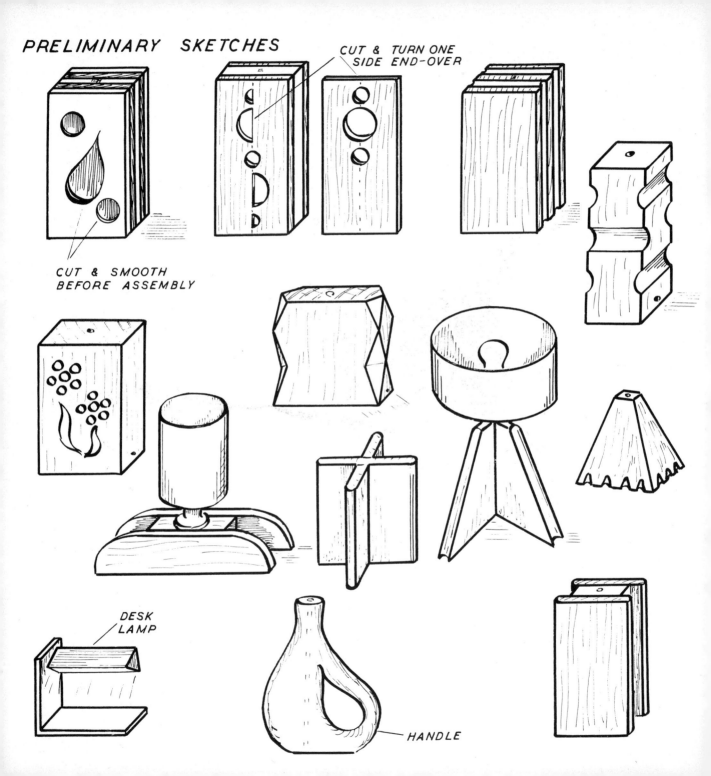

PRELIMINARY SKETCHES

CUT & TURN ONE
SIDE END-OVER

CUT & SMOOTH
BEFORE ASSEMBLY

DESK
LAMP

HANDLE

ABOVE LEFT The simple lamp base consists of laminations of maple and African mahogany, the holes being drilled and thoroughly smoothed before glueing the pieces together. ABOVE RIGHT The two lathe-turned lamps were designed and made by CSE candidates to use light and dark coloured woods for decorative effect. BELOW RIGHT An unusual lamp base. It was made by a fifth form pupil who had been looking at the 'erosion' carvings shown earlier.

ABOVE LEFT The large lamp base consists of a block of lovoa about 100 mm square and 350 mm tall. The lines are inlays of beech and the decoration is cut out of thin beech using a fret saw. The decorations were dyed black before mounting with glue. ABOVE RIGHT The flower lamp consists of small pieces of mahogany glued on a base of Douglas fir. The laminated lamp is in figured oak and mahogany, the mahogany being fluted. LEFT The small lamp base is made from parts of an old desk and forms a vehicle for the fish carved in mahogany.

82

CHESS PIECES

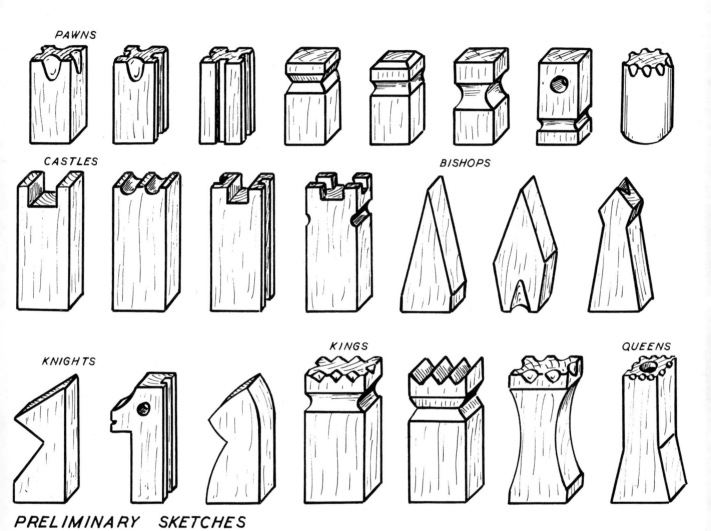

PAWNS

CASTLES   BISHOPS

KNIGHTS   KINGS   QUEENS

PRELIMINARY   SKETCHES

85

The making of wooden chess pieces gives great scope for practice and experience in simple design.

The two sets shown were made by twelve- to thirteen-year-old boys and an attempt has been made to retain some link with tradition and yet work with material and tools which may produce a variety of individual designs within a class. Beech was used for all pieces, one set being dyed when complete.

The sets also combine a box and a chess board, the lower one folds in the middle to close up, the upper one has the board on the sliding lid

BIRD BOXES AS A DESIGN PROJECT

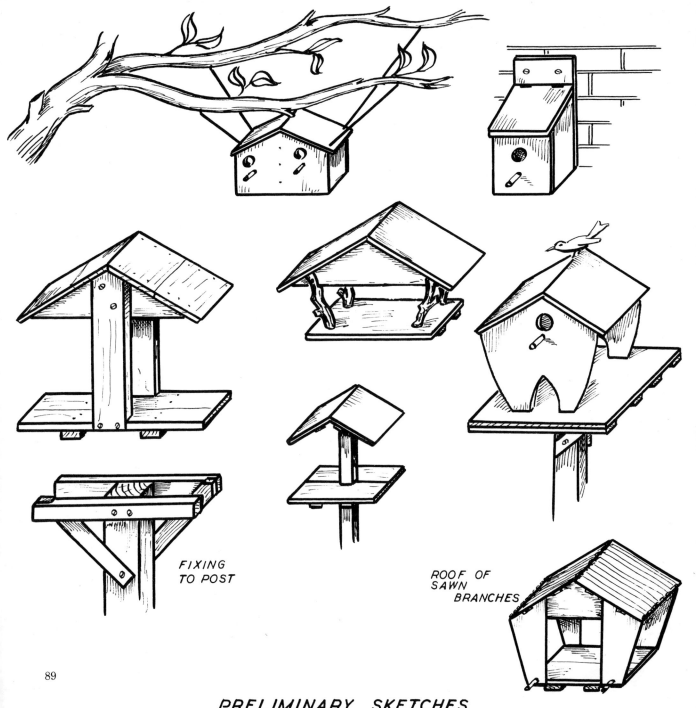

FIXING
TO POST

ROOF OF
SAWN
BRANCHES

89

PRELIMINARY SKETCHES

The making of nest boxes, bird tables or a combination of the two presents a very wide field for imaginative design.

The construction techniques involved can be very simple and the wood can be of very inferior quality. A waney edge left on the wood can often add charm and character.

The examples shown were made from a maple tree that fell down in the school grounds. When cut up the wood was found to be defective with fungus stains and with the canals formed by some species of grub. However, it served a useful purpose.

MISCELLANEOUS

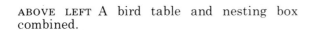

ABOVE LEFT A bird table and nesting box combined.

ABOVE RIGHT and RIGHT examples show the use of gouge cuts to accentuate the design. The leaf dish is divided into sections with gouge cuts left to indicate the vein structure of the leaf. The vase of flowers below has careful gouge cuts made to form the petal of each flower. The carving is made out of one piece of ash about 350 mm tall and 50 mm thick.

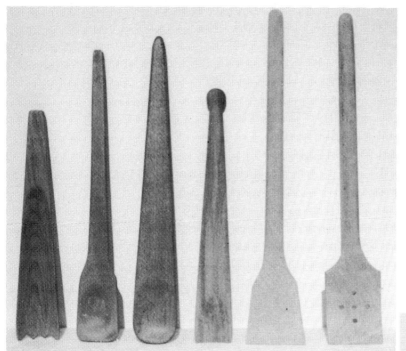

LEFT A variety of spoons and spatulas is shown. They were designed and made by eleven- and twelve-year-old pupils using beech. BELOW LEFT The bow-saw frame is made of red beech and the lathe-turned handles are made of ash in this example. The cord for tensioning the blade is of nylon and the metal rod for holding the blade is 6·3 mm diameter aluminium alloy. BELOW The wood-worker's mallet is made entirely of red beech. The metalworker's bossing mallet and tinman's mallet are made in red beech with ash handles.

An attempt is shown here to make wooden-soled sandals. The wood used is elm and the fitting of the foot is hollowed with a gouge and smoothed with a curved scraper. BELOW The heels on this pair are a separate piece of wood and the straps are of leather. ABOVE A slightly simpler pair of wooden sandals, the heel being carved from the one piece of wood.

The Conversion of Timber

Timber is a commodity of increasing cost. The last decade has seen a very steep price rise and it would be unrealistic to suppose that this trend will not continue or increase. This being so it is natural that every craftsman and every friend of every craftsman should show an eagerness to save and convert into useful timber every odd tree that formerly would have found its way onto the fire.

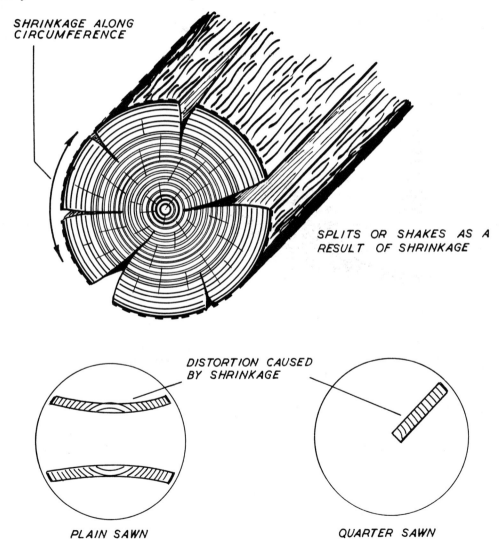

SHRINKAGE ALONG CIRCUMFERENCE

SPLITS OR SHAKES AS A RESULT OF SHRINKAGE

DISTORTION CAUSED BY SHRINKAGE

PLAIN SAWN

QUARTER SAWN

Efforts to save timber for useful purposes are sometimes frustrated through a lack of knowledge of how the wood will behave during drying out—the process known as seasoning. It is well to remember that a growing tree when cut down may contain up to half its weight in moisture which has to be dried out before the wood is fit to use. If this seasoning is not carefully controlled it is obvious that the wood will split on shrinkage.

A log when drying out does not shrink evenly in all directions and three directions of shrinkage have to be considered they are *Lengthwise, Along the Radius* and *Along the Circumference*. Shrinkage along the length or along the grain is very small and it is not a considerable factor in seasoning. Radial shrinkage is considerable and will result in reduction in size and some distortion but does not usually create sufficient tension to cause splits. Shrinkage along the circumference is the greatest and if a log is left in the round the drying and shrinkage of the outside is sufficient to cause large and deep splits all round the log.

In order to prevent large splits developing the log should be cut into pieces which will allow shrinkage without damage. This alone is not enough, the drying out of the surface must be slowed down in order to allow the drying out of the inside to keep pace. A very wet interior combined with a dry surface would again set up tensions resulting in smaller splits. The usual way of controlling the surface drying is by building the sawn wood into stacks each board being separated by a small strip of wood known as a *Sticker*. The speed of drying is to some extent controlled by the thickness of the stickers, the thinner they are the less air can circulate. It is also common practice to paint the ends of the boards as this reduces evaporation and prevents splitting. The stack should preferably be built in a covered open shed and raised off the ground. Felled timber which is unseasoned is subject to many types of insect and fungus attack and timber left drying on the ground is almost certain to be attacked. A white piece of sycamore can be completely spoiled for craft work by the grey stain left as a result of fungus growth during seasoning.

The seasoning of timber is a slow process and it is frequently said that for natural air seasoning an allowance of one year should be made for each 25 mm thickness of the wood. Needless to say this rule is not always strictly adhered to.

The above description of seasoning applies to the craftsman who has a small tree which he wishes to convert for his own use. Commercially timber is generally dried or part dried in a kiln. This process is very much quicker, taking weeks rather than years. The cut timber is stacked on a truck which is moved into a kiln where the timber is treated with steam and dry warm air alternately and this very quickly reduces the

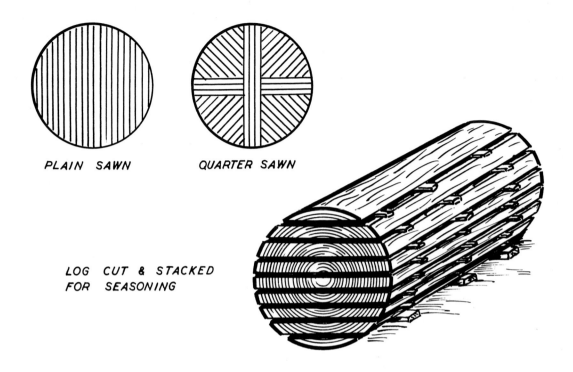

PLAIN SAWN   QUARTER SAWN

LOG CUT & STACKED
FOR SEASONING

moisture content of the wood. Kiln seasoned timber can be dried more fully than timber that is seasoned naturally and thus it is more suitable for use in centrally heated buildings, however, some hardwoods need partial air seasoning before they can be kiln dried.

Commercially timber is converted in one of two ways: the log may be plain sawn and as this involves a series of parallel cuts it is the method usually employed. Alternatively the log is quarter cut and this would be done either to produce boards of 'figured' oak or to reduce the distortion of the board on drying.

The craftsman converting his own tree would probably have to hire or borrow a chain saw. For craft work it is unlikely that lengths of more than 1 metre or $1\frac{1}{2}$ metres would be required and the first step therefore would be to make transverse cuts—that is across the log—to reduce it to moveable size. Cuts can then be made along the length and for this purpose, if the log is heavy enough to stand still, the log may be stood on end. A chain saw is a somewhat crude tool and it is not always easy to follow a line, but a sharp chain correctly ground is important and it is helpful to make all the cuts most of the way before finishing any of them, the whole log then stands still while the cuts are made. Chain saws are dangerous and must, of course, be used with great care.

The growth of a tree is outwards from the centre and each year a new layer of growth is added which is revealed as an *Annual Ring*. The ring is formed by the large pale spring and summer growth next to a darker thinner ring of autumn growth. Some tropical trees which have a constant growth rate do not show annual rings.

The roots collect moisture from the ground and pass this up the tree along the *Sapwood* to the leaves where the action of sunlight and the carbon dioxide in the air changes it into suitable plant food to feed the growing cells. This plant food returns along a thin layer called the *Bast* which is situated under the bark and feeds the growing cells in the *Cambium Layer*. The centre part of the tree the *Heartwood* is dead. In a felled tree it is often a different colour usually darker than the sapwood. As the sapwood contains more sugar it is more likely to be consumed by insects or fungus

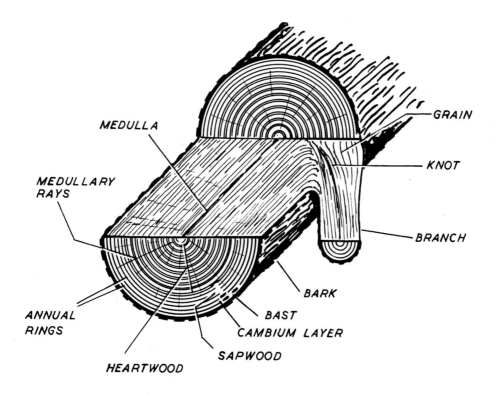

which, after all, are interested in the wood as a source of food. The cells of which the tree is composed are mostly arranged vertically to move sap or plant food up or down, but some cells are formed to radiate from the centre which is called the *Pith* or *Medulla* and these cells are called *Medullary Rays*.

The *Grain* or the fibres which form the grain of a piece of wood are vertical in the trunk and run along the length of the branches. It follows that when a branch grows from the trunk of a tree there is going to be some twisting of the fibres and this is called a knot. In softwood trees the branches frequently die and break off and the result will be a dead knot. Although the fibres which form the grain are strong lengthwise and can be cut to form shavings, they are not very well held together. A piece of wood, therefore is strong lengthwise but across its width it is quite weak. When a board is cut with part of the outside of the tree remaining on it this is said to be a *Waney Edge* and the small splits which often develop in timber are called *Shakes*.

The quality of timber will depend mainly, of course, upon the type of tree that the timber comes from, but to a certain extent it will also depend upon the age of the tree and the conditions of growth. One of the attractions of working wood is that no two pieces are exactly the same and it is often possible to obtain great variations of colour texture and working qualities within one species.

Timber for Craft Work

ABURA This is a mild working close grained hardwood of a uniform pinkish colour. The wood does not have much character and is quite light in weight. Source — Equatorial Africa.

AFARA This is a light brown wood of average quality sometimes sold under the name IDIGBO. Source — Nigeria.

AGBA This is a very useful wood with a pleasant straight grain and a good texture — light brown in colour. It turns well and is suitable for small furniture but is rather soft for carving. Source — Tropical Africa.

ALDER This is not a particularly attractive wood. It is dull grey in colour and at one time was used for making clogs. Source — homegrown.

APPLE This is a very tough wood with an attractive grain and a pleasant pinkish colour. It is suitable for turning and tool making, particularly mallet heads. Source — homegrown.

ASH This is a valuable carving wood particularly when the clearly defined grain formed by the dark annual rings can be used as an attractive feature. The wood is well known for its 'elastic' qualities hence its use in handles for tools which require to be springy. The character of the wood varies considerably with the age of the tree. Source — homegrown.

ASPEN This is a species of POPLAR which provides a soft, lightweight and rather poor quality wood. Source—homegrown.

BALSA This wood is the lightest in weight obtainable hence its use for flying model aircraft. As it is very soft requiring only simple tools it is used extensively for making small models and for very early craft work. Source—South America.

BEECH This is a fine close grained wood of good quality. It is obtainable as RED BEECH or as WHITE BEECH—the former being somewhat harder. It is used for carving, turning, making wooden tools or tool handles and for furniture. Quarter cut beech shows a small 'figure' caused by the medullary rays. Source—Europe.

BIRCH This is a white close grained mild working wood that is suitable for very many purposes when obtainable. Commercially it is used for the manufacture of plywood. Source—Canada, Europe.

BOX This is a very dense hard close grained wood that is yellow in colour. It can be used for inlay, small carvings and turnings etc. English box is generally too small to be much use—the tree is extremely slow growing—the wood mainly comes from Turkey.

CEDAR The best known of the cedars is the American WESTERN RED CEDAR. It is a softwood of reddish brown colour known mainly for its durability hence its use in house building. The tree grows to a very large size. CENTRAL AMERICAN CEDAR known for its fragrance is a hardwood that is seldom found except perhaps as cigar boxes.

CHERRY This tree provides a very pleasant medium hard brown wood that is used mainly for carving and lathe turning. Source—homegrown.

CHESTNUT Timber under this name is the sweet chestnut and it provides a very useful brown wood sometimes mistaken for oak, however, it does not yield 'figure'. It is durable and easily cleft—hence its use in fencing. The so-called horse chestnut or conker tree provides an inferior softer wood which is not much used. Source — homegrown.

CYPRESS This is a softwood of average quality though considered to be durable, it is a yellowish brown colour. Source — U.S.A., East Africa.

DEAL This is a term used to describe any form of softwood, that is, wood that comes from a coniferous tree. Deal is often subdivided into red deal and white deal the latter being generally softer.

DOUGLAS FIR Sometimes known as OREGON PINE. It is a very good quality softwood with clear annual rings giving a well defined grain. The wood is strong, straight grained and it planes and works well. Source — U.S.A., British Columbia.

EBONY This is a hard dense black wood seldom used — though other woods are often 'ebonized'. Source — Africa, India.

ELM This timber is obtainable in several types the WYCH ELM being considered the best. It yields a coarse brown wood though the sapwood is often yellow. It is very resistant to splitting. The wood is perhaps best known for its use in gable boards, coffins and outdoor furniture, but for craft work it can be used for turning, carving and for furniture which features the use of wide boards. The tree in England faces extinction due to the spread of Dutch elm beetle which infects the tree with a fungus fatal to it. Source — Europe, Japan.

FIR This is a name often given to types of pine tree, for example, Scots pine or Scots fir, Douglas fir or Oregon pine.

GABOON This is a rather soft pink mahogany type wood. It is used commercially to make plywood but is also used for some craft work. Source — Tropical West Africa.

GUM This term is usually applied to the various species of eucalyptus tree from Australia.

103

HEMLOCK This is a softwood that owing to the clearly defined annual rings has a distinguished grain. Source — U.S.A., Canada.

HICKORY This is a good quality hardwood with 'elastic' properties hence its use for sports goods and hammer handles. It is whitish yellow and very similar to ash. Source — U.S.A., Canada.

HOLLY This tree provides a very dense white hardwood which is seldom obtainable and then only in small sizes. Source — homegrown.

HORNBEAM This is a tough greenish white wood that is not very often used. Source — homegrown.

IDIGBO This is a yellow brown mild working hardwood that is often used for educational and craft work. Source — Tropical Africa.

IMBUYA This wood sometimes called Brazilian walnut or Embuia is a very pleasant brown wood which sometimes contains streaks of a darker colour. It is quite a useful craft timber. Source — Brazil.

IROKO This wood sometimes called African teak though it does not have the same properties as Burma teak is a brown wood which is very suitable for all forms of craft work. Source — Nigeria.

JARRAH This is a dark red wood of the eucalyptus species from Australia.

JELUTONG This is a pale lightweight wood sometimes used for craft work. Source — East Indies.

KOKRODUA This is a species of Afromosia somewhat similar in appearance to teak that is dark brown in colour. It is a useful craft timber. Source — Tropical West Africa.

LABURNUM This tree provides a green coloured wood seldom used but considered to be suitable for small work. It is quite hard. Source — homegrown.

LARCH This tree provides a tough red and very durable wood. It is often used for outdoor work. It has a tendency to warp and twist. Source —homegrown.

LUAN This timber is generally red in colour and seldom found except in the form of plywood. A pale pink variety is also known. Source — Philippine Islands.

LIGNUM VITAE This is an extremely hard dark brown wood which is very heavy, it sinks in water. It may be used for turned or carved ornaments or for engineering work. Source—Tropical South and Central America.

LIME This is quite a soft, smooth, close grained wood. It is useful for early carving and other craft work, however, it is too soft to retain much detail. Source—homegrown.

LOVOA This wood frequently called African walnut is a pleasant mild working golden brown wood. It is obtainable in large sizes and is suitable for general work as well as lathe turning and carving. The dust provokes sneezing. Source—Tropical West Africa.

MAHOGANY Central American mahogany which may come from Cuba, Honduras, Costa Rica, Mexico or Panama is a rich red wood of excellent quality. Mahogany from this region is considered the best and it has been widely used for furniture making.

African mahogany is very similar to Central American though somewhat inferior, however, it is very suitable for all craft work when a red coloured wood is required.

MAKORE This rich red wood may sometimes pass under the name of Cherry mahogany. It tends to be harder and heavier than African mahogany. It makes very good turned bowls. Source—Nigeria, Ghana.

MANSONIA This is a dark grey close grained and mild working hardwood. It is very pleasant for craftwork but sometimes avoided as the dust tends to irritate. Source — Ghana, Nigeria.

MAPLE The homegrown tree provides quite a pleasant mild wood of a pinkish colour. The maple used commercially would generally be imported from North America. Birds eye maple is considered an attractive spotted grain formation which is caused by an infection of the tree resulting in an unnatural growth.

MELAWIS This is another name for RAMIN.

MERANTI This is a red timber of rather a coarse texture. It is liable to split and warp, however, it can be used for craft work. Source — Malaya.

OAK There are very many species of oak and for craft work the Japanese oak is favoured as it is generally mild working. For outdoor work homegrown oak is hard to better. Baltic oak is tough and reliable and Silky oak (which is not a true oak) from Australia is considered attractive.

Oak is a tough durable brown wood. It is perhaps best known for the clearly defined 'figure' caused by the large clusters of medullary rays exposed on quarter cut oak.

OBECHE This is a lightweight creamy white coloured wood of a rather soft and cork like nature. It is sometimes used for early craft work even though the grain is sometimes twisted and difficult to work. Source — Tropical West Africa.

PARANA PINE This is a timber of excellent working qualities and the attractive grain often with pink streaks is very popular. The wood is readily obtainable often in quite large sizes. Source — South America.

PINE This name covers a multitude of woods such as Alaskan pine (hemlock), Oregon pine (Douglas fir), Baltic pine (Red deal), Parana pine, Scots pine (Scots fir), Weymouth pine (Yellow or White pine), Pitch pine etc. Generally when referring to pine in this country the

Scots pine is meant and this is quite a tough durable softwood. It has a tendency to contain black dead knots when the wood comes from the upper part of the tree.

PLANE   Sometimes called the London plane produces a light brown wood of average quality.

PLUM   When obtainable the wood—usually in quite small sizes—can be useful for craft work. It is light brown in colour often with darker streaks. Source—homegrown.

POPLAR   There are several varieties of poplar and in general they provide a soft and rather inferior wood. An exception, however, is the North American Yellow poplar sometimes sold as American whitewood. Other types of poplar would probably be homegrown.

RAMIN   This is a very useful craft timber. It is straight grained, quite hard and reliable and of quite a pleasant creamy white colour. Commercially it is often used for dowels and mouldings. Source—Sarawak.

RAULI   This is often called Rauli beech or Chilean beech because of its similarity to European beech. It is quite a useful timber though with a tendency to split. Source—South America.

REDWOOD   Although Baltic pine is sometimes called redwood this term is generally used when referring to sequoia.

ROSEWOOD   The two main sources of this wood are Central and South America and East India. The wood is hard and decorative and a rich brown in colour.

SAPELE   This is one of the West African red mahogany type timbers. It is obtainable in large sizes often with a striped grain which is difficult to work by hand. Source—Tropical West Africa.

SEQUOIA   This is often considered the grandest tree in the world. It is a very ancient species which grows mainly in California. The tree grows to an enormous size and age. The wood is quite soft in texture, easy to work and durable.

SPRUCE This timber is often known as whitewood or White deal. There are many varieties of spruce tree one of the most attractive of which is the sitka or Silver spruce. It is a fast growing coniferous tree which provides joinery timber and wood pulp. The nature of the tree is to grow a main trunk with very many small side branches and this results in many knots particularly in the upper part of the tree. The 'softwood' on sale in any wood shop would probably be a variety of spruce. Source — Canada, Scandinavia.

SYCAMORE This tree provides a very pleasant medium hard and very white wood which is most useful for all forms of craft work. It frequently has an attractive ripple grain particularly in the lower part of the tree. Source — Homegrown.

TEAK True teak comes from Burma and India. It is a brown wood of exceptional character. It has been used for ship making and science benches because of its very durable character. Although prized for craft work it has a serious blunting effect upon tools and the wood works with a 'greasy' feel.

UTILE This rich red mahogany type wood is very useful for all forms of craft work including carving and turning. It produces a good finish without much trouble and polishes well. Source — West Africa.

WALNUT When obtainable European walnut is a most valuable craft timber, ideal for furniture or carving. It has a rich brown colour often tinged with dark grey and it is reasonably hard and of good texture.

More easily obtainable is AFRICAN WALNUT which often passes under the name of Lovoa. Also obtainable are American Black walnut and Caucasian walnut.

WHITEWOOD American whitewood — sometimes called Yellow poplar or basswood is a mild straight grained wood quite suitable for early craft work. It is more yellow than white in colour and it is often obtainable in wide boards. Source — U.S.A., Canada.

WILLOW There are several species of homegrown willow most of which yield a rather poor quality wood. However, the species sometimes called the 'cricket bat' willow has one useful purpose as its name implies. The wood is creamy white in colour.

YEW The Yew tree is interesting in that it is a needle leafed tree which bears berries and although classified as a softwood it is extremely hard. Commercially it is scarcely obtainable but when obtained the heartwood is red the sapwood being considerably paler. Small sizes only can be obtained and the wood is suitable for carving or when used with the waney edge for making name or number plates. Source — homegrown.

Equipment

It would, of course, be very nice to have a large supply of first class equipment available for our use before we start work. Our work would undoubtedly be easier if we had a bright workshop fitted with power tools and hand tools of every conceivable refinement. In actual fact most of us have to work in conditions and with equipment that are less than ideal and it is indeed possible to produce excellent work with a small amount of quite primitive tools.

We must have some kind of quite solid workbench. This should be fitted with a vice — preferably a woodworkers vice — as large as possible. Some method of holding wood on top of the bench is also required and this can be a large G cramp, a bench holdfast and, if any large carvings are to be made, a bench screw is also useful. A bench hook is required for holding wood when making small cuts.

Some saws are essential. It would be difficult to get by without a Ripsaw for work along the grain, a Cross-cut saw for work across the grain and a Tenon saw for small cuts. A Bow saw is essential — these are quite easily home-made — and a Coping saw is useful for curved cuts in thin wood.

A complete set of carving chisels is a useful luxury but it is possible to do a great deal with two chisels and two firmer gouges in narrow and medium widths. A mallet is, of course, essential but these are also quite easily home-made.

For shaping and finishing work the various 'surform' files are extremely useful. The round one is probably the most useful. The rasp is rather a poor substitute for the surform though it has a longer life. Various sizes of half round and round files are useful for finishing and a file card for cleaning these is a necessity.

Some drilling of holes is always necessary whether carving or modelling. A plain brace with a variety of bits, including a countersink, will drill holes in the larger sizes and a hand drill with a variety of drills will take care of the smaller sizes.

It is almost certain that a plane will at some time be needed and this should certainly be a metal one for ease of adjustment. The use of nails and screws will sometimes be required so a hammer (about 340 g) and a pair of pincers are needed. A large and small screwdriver and a bradawl will be required for screws. When model making a few joints are required so it would be helpful to have a try square and marking gauge. We assume that everyone has a rule.

Various types of glue are obtainable and modern glues if used correctly are very good. Possibly the two most useful are P.V.A. (Polyvinyl Acetate) — this comes in the form of ready-to-use white liquid and Cascamite (Resin) — this comes in the form powder which is mixed with water to form a waterproof glue. The main difference in use between the two is that P.V.A. dries to a hard flexible plastic which under strain can be subject to 'creep' whereas cascamite forms a hard glassy waterproof bond but the glue once mixed does not keep.

A supply of glasspaper or garnet paper is required for finishing. Paints, polishes and waxes are also needed to suit the work produced.

With this basic kit it is possible to start work and additions can be made when possible. There are very many books which deal thoroughly with the care and maintenance of tools so the subject is not dealt with here. It is sufficient to say that a blunt tool can never do its job properly and that tools if cared for will often last several lifetimes.